M.T. THOMPSON

The Guide to Self-Love

Master Your Morning Routine to Unlock Your True Potential for Inner Peace, Happiness, and Success

Second edition

This book was professionally typeset on Reedsy.
Find out more at reedsy.com

To my daughters, Lala and my soon-to-arrive little one, you are the embodiment of pure love, and my deepest wish is for you to grow up embracing your unique beauty and strength. May this book be a part of the legacy I leave you, a guide to the love that already exists within.

And most of all, to my Dad. Though you may no longer be here physically, I feel you guiding me every day—leading me toward my highest self and bringing me back to my path. I dedicate this to you with all my love & gratitude

"Owning our story and loving ourselves through that process is the bravest thing we'll ever do."

BRENÉ BROWN

Contents

Acknowledgments

Thank you to my love, Shola. You have always been my #1 supporter, and if it weren't for you, I wouldn't be where I am today. Thank you for helping make my biggest blessings, Lala and our soon-to-be little one. They are a huge reason I came back to this project.

I'd like to thank my friend, Dale Allen, for his help proofreading my original manuscript. He critiqued my style, helped me get my message across more clearly, and was a huge support mechanism.

My parents, as well, were instrumental in reminding me how much I loved to write. They helped me from a young age by allowing me to express myself by journaling. Before my dad passed away, he read an old journal of mine where I took notes on online marketing and how to be an author. My mom told me he couldn't wait to give it to me and tell me how proud he was that I had followed my dreams.

Finally, I'd like to thank my longest friend, Bridget Kastl, for all of the love, support, and reminders of my worth. She has been a huge catalyst in my self-love journey. She helped in the process of the first edition of this book five years ago and again today in 2024. We are each other's accountability partners, and

I can't imagine life without her friendship.

Foreword: "The Guide to Self-Love" By Ameer Abdullah

"Hold fast to dreams, for if dreams die, life is a broken-winged bird that cannot fly" – Langston Hughes. Growing up as a child, I always dreamt of playing in the NFL. My imagination would run rampant thinking about all the possibilities that playing in the NFL would bring. While all the other kids watched cartoons, I was watching highlights of my favorite players. When my siblings asked for electronics for the holidays, I asked for football equipment. I even dedicated an entire second grade career day presentation, in which my parents were present, to explaining the entire process of how I was going to become a professional football player. Needless to say, my road to the NFL wasn't as simple and conventional as it was presented that day in the second grade.

Heading into my fifth year in the NFL, I can honestly say that each year has presented its own unique challenge that has shaped me into the man I am today. I'm very familiar with the up and down roller coaster that life can cast upon us. In only my second year in the NFL I tore my Lisfranc ligament in my left foot, which supports balance and explosion in the foot. To repair my foot, I had to get two surgical screws placed into my foot and I couldn't walk on it for 4 months. I was completely devasted by the injury. I had become that broken-winged bird. In the wake of this injury I had lost faith in myself, I had lost faith in my dreams, and ultimately, I had lost self-love. That young bright-eyed boy who never stopped dreaming had vanished and only self-doubt and reluctancy existed. Be grateful for the contrasts of life, because it could be those very moments that introduce something very special to your life.

I took up yoga a few months after being able to walk again and this is where I met Melinda Thompson. Upon first meeting Melinda I knew right away that this young woman was special. She only spoke positive things, there was no hesitation in her speech, she truly believed every word that was spoken from her mouth. This was a quality that I had never seen before and honestly because I was suffering from so much self-doubt from my previous injury, it was a quality that I needed in my life. When we first met, Melinda was working as a personal yoga instructor in the city of Detroit, where the beginning of her ambition was truly born. Melinda would spend hours on the road each day traveling to clients all over southeastern Michigan, spreading her love for yoga, while also spreading her loving influence on those she came in contact with. The Intention in which she moved with each day became contagious to be around and it lifted me out of a very negative space. In our yoga sessions not only did I improve physically, I improved spiritually. Melinda always picked me up when I was down, but also would challenge me when I most needed it. Little did I know those yoga sessions would shape a much deeper and fulfilling focus in my life, the importance of self-love.

Prior to adopting yoga into my lifestyle and meeting Melinda, I did not understand self-love. I had only viewed love as something you could receive or give to an exterior presence. I did not have the contraceptive to understand that it takes the genuine indulgence in self-love before we can even begin to give or receive love. Melinda would always repeat the same Mantra at the end of each of our yoga sessions, "You are worthy". These words remain with me today and serve as a reinforcement that loving yourself is the first step to achieving anything. We live in a world where often times it isn't encouraged to love ourselves. Self-love is often misinterpreted as conceited or self-centered, however, in actuality self-love is the birth place of individuality and understanding your purpose. I'm fortunate to have watch firsthand the evolution of Melinda Thompson, from the bubbly yoga instructor in Detroit to the now thriving business yogi and author in Los Angeles.

Melinda's Guide To Self-Love provides an opportunity for its readers to reconnect with themselves and to learn the powerful values that come from embodying self-love. This book gives a concise structural template that will naturally eliminate all self-judgment and self-reluctance that you have within yourself. Melinda vulnerably expresses the truths of her personal maturation, humanizing the process of achieving self-love. There is nothing worth having in this world that doesn't come without a struggle, and the authenticity of this book highlights the importance of implementing structure to one's life on the path of self-love. Self-love is constant and as your circumstances change, so too will your values. No matter what turns the path to -self-love gives you, always remember YOU ARE WORTHY!

Ameer practicing his mindfulness before Las Vegas Raiders away game against the Baltimore Ravens at M&T Bank Stadium. Taken by Michael Clemens/Las Vegas Raiders

Las Vegas Raiders running back Ameer Abdullah (8) during the regular season away game against the Baltimore Ravens at M&T Bank Stadium

Prologue

To the ones seeking peace within and learning to fall in love with every part of themselves. Brave souls daring to break cycles, rewrite stories, and claim a life filled with purpose, joy, and self-acceptance, I am so excited you found this book. However it came to you, whether it was on social media, a friend, or you just stumbled across it, you've found the trailhead of the path to self-love and happiness. Every book I have read seemed to have popped out of nowhere—exactly when I needed it most. They sustained me on my path. They helped me get through whatever struggles or blocks I was experiencing. I hope this book finds you in the same way.

It's difficult for me to finish books that are too long and meandering. My favorite books are clear, concise, and rich with valuable information—but also to the point and not too filled with fluff. Books that I can reopen at any point on my journey and get re-inspired in a new way. The meaning of the exact words and concepts change as we continue to grow along our journey. This is why I'm writing this book (and why I re-wrote it 5 years later)—it is a distillation of the ideas and philosophies that have helped me reach a beautiful place of peace and self-love.

The universe hands you words of wisdom and knowledge at the

perfect time. It's no accident that you came across this guide. It's here to help you grow, flourish, and realize your tremendous self-worth. Life is meant to be spent loving ourselves. To find peace and happiness, we must take daily steps to improve our overall mental health.

In the following pages, I will challenge you to take action every morning and take the necessary steps to become the most lovable version of yourself. This will allow you to break free from the negative thoughts that your ego feeds you and find the self-love that your spirit has been waiting for. I'll guide you through journal prompts to help you identify your 'why,' discover positive affirmations and gratitude, and visualize your dream life. This will help you speak your dreams into reality with a new level of potency and confidence.

Learning how to love myself began when I started doing yoga. Yoga has helped me in many ways, but the most valuable is that it has taught me how to *love* myself. Before starting my yoga practice, I didn't treat myself with love and respect. I was in a job that I didn't love, a stagnant relationship, and I surrounded myself with people who reinforced my low self-esteem. This all began to change when I started my yoga practice in 2012. As my body became stronger and more flexible and my mind became calmer and more focused, I noticed how I viewed myself also changed. Rather than allowing myself to be defined by the views of others, I realized that my identity came from within. I was in control of my thoughts, actions, and beliefs. I realized that I wanted to change them for the better. This unexpected benefit of yoga has become the most valuable.

There are many books on yoga out there that discuss its physical and mental benefits. However, few talk about how yoga can actually change the trajectory of one's life. For me, yoga was the beginning of a profound personal transformation. I developed powerful morning habits and routines that set the stage for a mindful, purposeful day. I call this practice the 'Magic Morning,' inspired by the book "The Miracle Morning" by Hal Elrod. I'm excited to share this practice with you! Thank you for trusting me to help guide you.

Introduction

In this book, you're embarking on a journey—a journey of self-love, discovery, and peace within. You hold in your hands not just a book but a guide to understanding yourself in deeper, more compassionate ways. Whether you're here to find clarity in your purpose, strengthen your self-worth, or learn tools for a more mindful, fulfilling life—each chapter is designed to support you on your unique path.

The chapters ahead will introduce you to practices and mindsets that have the power to transform how you see yourself and the world around you. You'll explore the art of daily affirmations and the strength of simple yet powerful words like 'I am.' You'll learn how to cultivate gratitude, wake up with intention, and go with the flow of life's ever-changing currents. These practices will help you build a strong foundation, reconnecting you with your value and capacity to create the life you desire.

We'll also dive into practical tools for living with purpose and tapping into the power of visualization and manifestation. These aren't just theoretical ideas; they are grounded in the wisdom of psychology and self-care practices that have helped countless others. As you move through each chapter, I encourage you to experiment, reflect, journal, and make each concept your own.

Ultimately, this book is an invitation to reconnect with the incredible power that lies within you. You are capable of more than you may realize, and as you apply these practices, you'll begin to unlock new levels of self-acceptance, resilience, and joy. This journey is yours, and every chapter you turn is a step closer to the life you were meant to live. I hope this book serves as a companion, guiding you back to yourself and encouraging you to embrace all that you are and all that you are becoming. Take your time, revisit sections as needed, and trust the process.

* * *

I have broken up the 'Magic Morning' into 8 limbs, which I derived from the 8 limbs of yoga, which are:

1. Yama - attitude towards environment.
2. Niyama - attitude towards ourselves.
3. Asanas - physical postures.
4. Pranyama - the breath.
5. Pratyahara - withdrawl of the senses.
6. Dharana - concentration.
7. Dhyana - meditation.
8. Samadhi - complete integration.

This is not a book on yoga. But rather it's a book that has been inspired by my yoga practice.

The 8 limbs of the Magic Morning are:

1. Wake up early
2. Read empowering literature
3. Meditate
4. Speak mantras
5. The gratitude journal
6. Visualization
7. Move your body
8. Integration

If you're new to these concepts - don't worry. You're not alone, and everyone starts somewhere. This is a guide to ultimately help you find self-love by focusing on YOU - putting yourself first by waking up before having to be anywhere to write, speak out loud, and visualize your dreams into existence. If you're not new to these concepts, I hope my version and my experiences resonate with you to see things in a new way. I truly hope something clicks for you that hasn't clicked in the past.

You'll hear about my personal experiences doing so in my life and the times I wasn't on my path because of outside influences and not trusting my intuition—which is one of the most important things you can do on your path to living your purpose.

At the end of the book, you'll find the Magic Morning guide as a reference for your journal prompts and an example of my personal journal prompt. While I don't know exactly where you are in your personal development, I'm certain that you'll achieve the self-love and happiness you're dying to find by following the daily routine that has shaped me into the woman I am today.

My mission in life is to help others find the self-love, confidence, and positivity that I have worked hard to achieve for myself. Every moment I stop and smile with love for my life, I often wish for others to feel the same amount of joy I feel in my heart. I have cultivated such a powerful level of love and light for life, that God/the universe is guiding me to impact more and more people. You'll see that I refer to 'Source' in different ways throughout the book to resonate with as many of you as I can. Whatever you believe in is who I am referring to. (:

I want each and every one of you to create this light for yourself. You will be rewarded for the rest of your life just by putting in the work now—no matter what stage of your life you're in. This work is internal, but you will shine externally without even trying. You will have a glow to you that people will notice. Doing these practices has shaped my body and cleared my skin—just by releasing unnecessary stress and doubts. If your physical body and skin are also things you are trying to improve... you will most definitely see changes.

I believe in you as much as I believe in myself. We are all the same. We are all capable. We are all worthy. It's just about focusing on the positive, going with the flow, and allowing law of attraction to take control. To eat the fruits that life has to offer, we must put in the labor of becoming the best versions of ourselves.

Are you ready to become the best version of yourself so you can attract every single person and thing that you've always dreamed of?! Then let's put in this work together.

1

Don't Worry, Be Happy

I'm beginning this book by exploring simple yet profound ways to enhance daily happiness, focusing on mindset shifts, gratitude, and the power of intentional living. I'll mention some of these things in greater detail as the book goes on, especially when we put them into practice. But before anything, I'd love for you to make the first entry in your journal, new or old, and title it "Self-Love Journey." Begin by making a list of all the things you love about yourself. Then, write down a list of things you want to release, that no longer serve you. Maybe any negative reoccurring thoughts that create downward spirals, or false statements you tell yourself about what other people think or how you may see yourself. Lastly, write down your intention while you're reading this. Write it with intention and close your eyes to feel it shift in you. Once we get into the daily routine part, you can actively repeat mantras of the things you're calling in and reinforce your mind to think more positively. I want you to actively take notes and write down as much as you can. I swear by writing. It makes it stick more in your brain if you re-read it after you write it down rather than just saying it out loud once.

Now that you have your intentions in place, let's get into some happiness techniques! The most important part of your self-love journey starts with inner peace and happiness. With these simple ways of making each day more mindful, you can create a safe haven within you:

Smile more

Happiness is often thought of as something we either have or don't, but in truth, it's a state of being we can actively cultivate through small, intentional actions. One of the simplest and most immediate ways to invite more happiness into your life is by smiling more often. Studies show that smiling, even when it feels forced, can boost your mood and signal to your brain that you're happy. Smiling also has a ripple effect, spreading positivity to those around you and fostering deeper connections.

Get outside as often as you can

One of my favorite ways to nurture happiness is by spending more time outdoors in nature. Going for a walk, getting to the beach in the summer/skiing in the winter, or simply sitting in your backyard while you drink your morning coffee, being in nature helps reduce stress, improve mental clarity, and elevate your mood. Fresh air, sunlight, and the calming sounds of the natural world are all tools to help you reset and find joy in the present moment.

This is a huge reason I love to practice yoga or do my at-home workouts in my backyard or at the beach. The feeling of the warmth from the sun, the slight breeze in the air, and the smell of fresh flowers or grass greatly affect your mood! You feel one with nature, one with everything around you. Especially if you do something active outside. The endorphins intensify the oneness you feel with Source. If you work a lot and don't get a lot of sunshine throughout the day, do your best to take breaks and walk outside!

Build Meaningful Connections

Human connection is one of the greatest predictors of happiness. Relationships—whether with friends, family, or partners—provide a sense of belonging and support. Nurturing these bonds and investing in meaningful connections can lead to a more fulfilling life. Positive relationships boost well-being and serve as a buffer against stress. Practice making an effort to connect with loved ones regularly. Schedule quality time, express appreciation, and prioritize active listening to deepen these bonds.

Spending more quality time with friends and family let us know we're not alone in our experiences. Similarly, stepping outside your comfort zone to try a new hobby, take a dance class, or learn a new skill can spark joy by reigniting your sense of curiosity and adventure. Challenging yourself in new ways builds confidence and brings a fresh perspective to life.

Exploration

Happiness often grows when we embrace a sense of exploration. Booking a trip to visit a new destination, whether it's a weekend getaway or a far-off adventure, opens your mind to different cultures, experiences, and landscapes. Travel enriches the soul, reminding you of the beauty and diversity in the world and how much there is to be grateful for. Each of these steps, while small, contributes to creating a life filled with greater joy, connection, and fulfillment. Happiness, after all, is not a destination—it's a practice. While life's ups and downs are inevitable, some practices and mindsets can help us cultivate lasting joy and resilience.

Embrace the Power of Positivity

Our mindset shapes our experience. Positive thinking doesn't mean ignoring challenges or difficult emotions, but it does mean training our minds to focus on the good vs the bad. By reframing negative situations and looking for silver linings, we build resilience and invite more joy into our lives! Research in positive psychology shows that maintaining a positive mindset can boost well-being and overall life satisfaction. Each morning, start your day with a positive affirmation or intention, like

14

"Today, I choose to see the good in each moment."

This small shift can set a positive tone and help you stay grounded, even when life throws curve balls. Once I started doing this, life became sweeter! I have to remind my friends and family: "It's going to be okay!" or "It's okay!" immediately after something bad happens because it always is! If you really think about it, there is ALWAYS a silver lining in every situation, even in really bad situations. As hard as life can be, make it a little easier by accepting it for what it is and looking at the bright side. Resilience is a powerful tool that has a lasting effect on our mental.

Cultivate Gratitude

Practicing gratitude consistently can shift our focus from what's lacking to what's abundant in our lives. Studies have shown that gratitude practices can increase overall happiness and decrease symptoms of depression. Practice: Write down three things you're grateful for each day. These can be as simple as a warm cup of tea, a supportive friend, or a beautiful sunset. This ritual rewires your brain to recognize and amplify positive experiences. My gratitude practice has truly changed my life. When you speak or write down what you're grateful for, more good things come to you. It's like you're telling God or the universe that you're not taking any blessings for granted and are ready for more blessings!

Practice Mindfulness

Mindfulness is the art of being fully present in each moment, accepting it without judgment. By engaging with our sur-roundings and savoring the little moments, we can find greater joy and peace. Mindfulness practices, such as meditation and mindful breathing, reduce stress and enhance mental clarity. Practice: Take five minutes daily to sit quietly, focus on your breath, and observe your thoughts without attachment. This simple exercise can improve focus and help you develop a greater sense of inner peace. I'll get more into this and all these topics in the next chapter by teaching you an easy morning routine that only takes 10 minutes for each exercise to make a huge shift in your life to make you feel happier, more confident, and more peaceful.

Prioritize Physical Wellness

Our physical well-being is intrinsically connected to our mental state. Engaging in regular exercise, eating a balanced diet, and getting sufficient sleep all contribute to a happier, healthier life. Physical activity, in particular, releases endorphins, which are natural mood lifters. Studies highlight that even 20 minutes of exercise a day can improve mood and reduce anxiety. Practice: Try incorporating movement you enjoy into your daily routine, whether it's yoga, dancing, or a walk. Listen to your body, nourish it with good food, and prioritize rest.

Practice Self-Compassion

Lastly, remember to be kind to yourself. Life is a journey, and mistakes and setbacks are part of it. Self-compassion involves treating yourself with the same kindness you would offer a friend. By embracing self-compassion, you allow yourself to grow without harsh self-criticism. When you experience a setback, pause and ask, "How would I support a friend going through this?" Extend that same understanding and encouragement to yourself.

Happiness isn't a destination; it's a continuous practice. Incorporating these habits and perspectives into your life creates a foundation for resilience and joy. Remember, each day offers new opportunities to cultivate happiness, and your small steps add up over time. Embrace the journey, and know that happiness is within reach!

2

Identify your 'WHY'

In a world that often pulls us in countless directions, it's easy to lose sight of our true desires, buried beneath the weight of expectations and obligations. Yet, within each of us lies a compass pointing towards our unique "why"— the driving force that fuels our happiness and gives life its deepest meaning. Identifying this "why" is not just a philosophical pursuit; it's the foundation of a fulfilling life. Please reflect on this as you read this book. You may still be living a purpose from your past. We're meant to grow and evolve throughout life, so make sure you reflect as often as possible to re-align with your Highest Self.

Living merely to meet the expectations of others or to fulfill basic necessities can lead to a life half-lived, where days blur into one another in a monotony of routine. But when we connect with our "why," we ignite a passion that illuminates our path. This purpose inspires us to rise each morning with a sense of excitement, knowing that we are living in alignment with our truest selves. Showing up for yourself means honoring your desires and dreams, even when they deviate from the conventional path. It requires the courage to listen to your inner voice and to prioritize what brings you joy. This journey of self-discovery and actualization empowers you to craft a life that feels authentically yours.

By embracing your "why," you begin to navigate life with intention, making choices that resonate with your core values. This alignment fosters a sense of fulfillment that transcends momentary pleasures or superficial successes. It encourages you to step off the treadmill of societal norms and to create a rhythm that is uniquely yours. This might mean pursuing a passion project, cultivating meaningful relationships, or simply allowing yourself the freedom to explore what brings you joy.

It's important to remember that your "why" can evolve. As you grow and change, so too might your sources of happiness and fulfillment. Embrace this fluidity, allowing yourself the grace to adapt and realign with your evolving aspirations. By doing so, you continually recommit to a life of purpose, passion, and profound fulfillment, ensuring that each day is not just lived but truly savored.

Understanding the underlying reasons behind our actions—our "why"—is fundamental to personal growth and fulfillment. Identifying this core motivation provides clarity, direction, and a sense of purpose, guiding us through life's challenges and decisions. Human behavior is influenced by a complex interplay of factors, including biological drives, psychological needs, and social influences. Theories such as Maslow's Hierarchy of Needs suggest that individuals are motivated to fulfill basic physiological needs before progressing to higher-level psychological desires, culminating in self-actualization. Similarly, Self-Determination Theory posits that autonomy, competence, and relatedness are essential components driving human behavior.

Identifying one's "why" involves introspection and self-awareness. Engaging in reflective practices, like journaling or meditation, can help uncover personal values and passions. Additionally, seeking feedback from trusted individuals can provide external perspectives that illuminate intrinsic motivations. By aligning actions with core values and understanding the reasons behind our choices, we can lead more authentic and satisfying lives.

My favorite way to make sure I'm journaling on the regular is having a journal that is physically appealing. It must get me excited to grab it and open it up to write. If you don't own a journal that you love, the journal I love and use is here: www.happynotesbook.com/?ref=1tgkhe6xxz

Reflection

What is your why? In other words, why do you do the things you do? What brings you joy each day? I want you to grab your journal and write another entry of what you believe your why is. Label this one as "MY WHY." Start by simply jotting down some things that light you up and what makes you the happiest. Then, reflect on what your present-day looks like. Are you doing the things you love daily? This is where you will re-evaluate how you spend most of your time. Your actions should ultimately lead to living your purpose through passion, determination to reach your goals, and being the best version of yourself. This may require you to cut out unnecessary time scrolling on social media, hitting the snooze on your alarm every morning, or binge-watching Netflix all the time.

For the rest of this book, I will be advising you to pull out your journal and write an entry. So, keep it close by, and enjoy every second of writing about your goals, visions, affirmations, and meditations.

3

'I AM'

"I AM' - the two most powerful words, for what you put right after them shapes your reality" ~ Bevan Lee

"I am" are the two most powerful words because they act as a mirror reflecting your inner reality into your external world. Every thought and declaration you make after these words set the tone for your mindset, behavior, and ultimately, your life. This is why speaking affirmations aloud with intention carries immense power. By saying "I am capable," "I am resilient," or "I am enough," you're training your subconscious mind to align with those beliefs. Neuroscientific studies have shown that repeated affirmations can create new neural pathways, effectively rewiring the brain to support more empowering thought patterns. Crazy, right?! It really does work. Notice the shifts in your life after implementing these practices.

Beyond shaping internal beliefs, "I am" statements have a ripple effect on your external reality. They dictate how you show up in the world—whether with confidence and self-assuredness or hesitation and self-doubt. When you consciously choose positive "I am" declarations, you're not just rewriting your internal narrative. Still, you're also giving the universe a clear message about the energy you're bringing to the table. As the law of attraction suggests, the energy you project is the energy you attract. Therefore, being intentional with your "I am" statements helps ensure that what you desire and believe aligns with what you manifest.

It's also worth exploring how "I am" connects to identity. When you declare something with "I am," it becomes part of your identity—who you perceive yourself to be. This aligns with the psychological principle of self-concept, which posits that individuals act in accordance with their beliefs about themselves. If you repeatedly tell yourself, "I am creative," for example, you're not just describing yourself—you're reinforcing a part of your identity. As this identity solidifies, it encourages behaviors and habits that support that belief. The result? A reality that reflects the identity you've chosen to embody. Look back at your lowest times in life—were you continuing the cycle by saying you're a failure? Or you don't deserve something because you didn't try hard enough? Think about a time where things flowed easily to you. I bet you were feeling very empowered and confident, which brought more opportunities easily to you.

With that being said, the power of "I am" also demands caution. Negative statements—"I am not good enough," "I am a failure"—carry just as much weight, if not more, because our minds are often more attuned to negativity. These statements become self-fulfilling prophecies, chaining us to limitations that don't reflect our true potential. It's vital to monitor our internal dialogue and replace limiting beliefs with empowering truths.

In essence, "I am" is both the starting point and the compass. It is the gateway to intentional living and the foundation of a reality shaped by purpose. The next time you say, "I am," pause. Reflect. Choose words that reflect your highest self and your wildest dreams. As the ancient proverb says, "As a man thinketh in his heart, so is he." Your thoughts, powered by the words "I am," hold the key to the life you desire.

You are that which you believe you are. This may be hard for some of you to realize or believe, but with every single thought you have and every time you speak something about yourself, the universe matches that frequency into manifestations. It's actually kind of scary to think about. Every time you say you're not good enough or something like, "Ugh, that person doesn't like me," or "I am not good enough for this position," you are speaking that reality into existence. Pay attention to your thoughts and only think and say kind things about yourself.

How often have you noticed someone get a raise or an opportunity they didn't deserve, at least on the surface? I guarantee the only difference between you and them is that they believed they were worthy and likely spoke words of affirmation to create that reality. Even if they weren't the best person for that opportunity or promotion, they acted like it, and they believed every ounce of themselves to be perfect for it. You, on the other hand, probably can think back to negative self-talk or worries that prevented you from even trying. The universe simply matched your frequency.

Moreover, the language we use not only impacts our internal state but also influences how others perceive and interact with us. Consistently expressing positive "I am" statements can attract supportive relationships and opportunities, creating a self-fulfilling cycle of positivity. Therefore, being mindful of our language, particularly self-referential statements, is crucial in crafting a reality that aligns with our aspirations and well-being.

Who likes to be around negative Nancy? I sure don't! I have to admit that I've let go of friends who have a bad habit of complaining about their lives or having negative comments to say about other people. If you don't have anything nice to say, don't say anything at all. It lowers your vibration to get stuck on others' success or path with judgment just because it's not *your* way of doing it, or speaking negatively about them to make yourself feel better. This is a huge 'ick' for me, being as positive and friendly as I am—it's hard to be around these types of people. Don't be that person.

In the next section of this book, I will share with you the 8 limbs of the Magic Morning, which include every exercise to do in the morning to become the highest version of yourself, both internally and externally. This includes speaking affirmations like the ones I mentioned above. Your mind doesn't know what is real or what is just a mantra. You need to highlight this and take notes. It's going to challenge you to watch your thoughts and watch your ego. The universe, and everything in it, is energy. This includes you. Your thoughts are just as real and impactful as your physical body. So, who are you? What version of you are you thinking into existence?

4

Magic Morning Routine

"Wake up early every day so that while others are still dreaming, you're making your dreams come true" - Hal Elrod

Creating a morning routine sets the tone for the rest of your day. The book that taught me this was "The Miracle Morning" by Hal Elrod. I reference practices I initially implemented into my morning routine from that book. I call my practice the Magic Morning because it has helped me to manifest a reality that I can only describe as magical. I could have never imagined that I'd be where I am today. I've arrived here by taking one morning at a time: focusing on my gratitude, my mind, body, and spirit. It gives me a special kind of energy and self-confidence that carries into my character as I interact socially with friends and family. It gave me this peaceful and uplifting aura that leaves lasting impressions. On the days where I hit snooze, or I sit and scroll on social media, I am limiting my potential.

Being a yogi for 12 years now, I can assure you that you'll

find so much peace by following this morning routine. The meditation part is probably going to be the most impactful part of this book; however, it might take you months or even years to figure that out. Meditation is a good example of enjoying the 'fruits of your labors' because sitting in silence and having the answers flow to you effortlessly takes a lot of time and work. Waking up and completing the magic morning is going to be difficult. It is for me! However, completing the exercises is not the goal; it's dedication that counts. That means if life happens and you don't get enough sleep the night before, or you can only commit to these exercises a couple times a week rather than every day, that's okay too. 2-3 times per week is better than not trying to do anything at all.

The reason I want you to complete these exercises right when you wake up in the morning is because it shapes the day completely how it's meant to be. When you wake up and are rushing to go somewhere without proper alone time to gather your thoughts, emotions, and intentions - you can potentially lose out on so many amazing surprises the universe wants to send you. Instead, you'll likely allow the ego to take control. This is when lack of confidence, or feelings of unworthiness are most likely to happen.

LIMB #1

WAKE UP ONE HOUR EARLIER

The reason why I started to LOVE this part of my journey to self-love was realizing how much of a bad ass I felt to be able to wake up before everyone else to put in work. It's a grind! On days where you go out with friends the night before, or you're on vacation, are the best mornings to wake up and put in personal development to let go of any thoughts of guilt.

Establishing a habit of waking up early offers numerous

benefits that can enhance both mental and physical well-being. Early risers often experience improved mood and increased productivity throughout the day. A study published in JAMA Psychiatry found that waking up just one hour earlier can reduce the risk of major depression by 23%. This shift in sleep timing aligns with our natural circadian rhythms, promoting better mental health.

Conversely, the common practice of hitting the snooze button may have unintended consequences. Research from the University of Notre Dame revealed that 57% of participants were habitual snoozers, a behavior linked to increased sleep disturbances and reliance on caffeine. While some studies suggest that brief snoozing might not significantly impact cognitive performance, the overall consensus indicates that relying on the snooze function can disrupt sleep patterns and reduce sleep quality. To cultivate a healthier sleep routine, it's advisable to set a consistent wake-up time and resist the urge to snooze. Implementing gradual changes, such as adjusting bedtime by 15-minute increments, can facilitate this transition. Additionally, exposure to natural morning light and engaging in early-day physical activity can reinforce the body's internal clock, making it easier to wake up feeling refreshed and alert.

One of the keys to this is eliminating the snooze button at all costs. The moment you decide to snooze is the moment you are saying to the universe you don't care about your goals. This one will always be a bit of a struggle for me, especially being a mom and having to get up multiple times in the night to tend to my baby, or nights that I just couldn't fall asleep and didn't get the sufficient amount sleep my body functions best from.

As hard as some mornings are, those are the mornings its most impactful to just jump out of bed and do what you planned to do the night before. You can always go to bed earlier the next night, or try to sneak in a nap if it's possible. There's just nothing like the morning hours of the day. It's the only time of the day when you have a complete blank sheet of paper, where you don't feel weighed down like you may later on in the day.

Having alone time in the morning to focus on ME, and only me, has literally changed my life. I can still think back and remember all of mornings I woke up and didn't want to get out of bed because the first thing I had on my schedule was school or work. Would you like the first thing on your schedule to be about YOU or would you like it to be about someone else?

Sure, your plans might be with family or loved ones or even a fun group activity... but wouldn't you rather walk into that room or that place around others with a glowing aura of LIGHT and confidence and excitement about what's going on internally?! This makes law of attraction an extremely beautiful thing when you work on your inner being so hard. Each week, you'll start to notice that you become more and more important in school, at work, and out in the world. You become more important because you are more valued. You become more valued because you believe in your own personal worth. How you view yourself is reflected to the world, and you should feel damn proud of the work you put in day in and day out.

It's not only about being awake an hour early, but it's what you do in that first hour that matters. No more laying in bed scrolling on Instagram or TikTok. No more comparing yourself to other people's lives. It's time to focus on being the best person you can be and cultivating more and more love for yourself than ever.

The next few pages are about defining your hopes and dreams and planning to turn them into reality. When you realign yourself with your purpose it's a fresh start. This will make you fall in love with yourself and life all over again.

LIMB #2

READ INSPIRATIONAL LITERATURE
"Books are a uniquely portable magic." – Stephen King

Incorporating daily reading of inspirational literature can significantly enhance one's mental and emotional well-being. Engaging with uplifting content fosters a positive mindset, reduces stress, and promotes personal growth. According to a 2022 article in Psychology Today, reading fiction improves social cognition and empathy, which are essential for building meaningful relationships and understanding others' perspectives.

Moreover, regular exposure to motivational texts can serve as a catalyst for self-improvement. Inspirational books often provide new perspectives and insights, encouraging readers to reflect on their lives and make positive changes. As noted by Linda Handley, such literature can help individuals gain new perspectives, find motivation, build resilience, reduce stress, and improve empathy.

Establishing a daily habit of reading inspirational literature not only enriches the mind but also contributes to a more fulfilling and purpose-driven life. By dedicating time each day to absorb positive messages, you can cultivate resilience, enhance emotional intelligence, and maintain a hopeful outlook, even in challenging times. This is a great way to rewire your brain like I mentioned before. What you think about most is what you ultimately believe in. When you're constantly reading inspiring words, learning from reputable people, you will begin to live the theories.

Growing up, I never liked reading, but I was a go-getter. At age 16, I was attending both high school and cosmetology school. My schedule was packed everyday. Not to mention cheerleading practices every day. But when I graduated high school, I finally had some time to stop and think. I found myself asking these questions: Who am I? What do I want? Do I continue working as a hairdresser? I enjoyed that work; I was making decent money, but deep down I knew it wasn't my purpose. It wasn't the thing that filled me with excitement and satisfaction that I knew was possible. I would talk about my love for yoga and its benefits to my clients than hair. I was in the beginning stages of my personal development journey.

This was when I began seeking for answers, trying to find my "why." This is when I discovered my love of reading. Each book and article became a "portable magic," guiding me along my journey. Serendipitously, the right books seemed to find their way to me. Each one seemed like a gift from God, given to me when I needed it most. When I found personal development books, my whole being lit up with joy, I could feel that they were leading me down the path to discovering my true purpose and who I wanted to become. In each sentence, I would stop and think about how I could contextualize it into my own life.

The first self-development book I read, that I was lucky enough to be gifted, was "Think and Grow Rich" by Napoleon Hill. This book introduced me to the concept of manifestation. *All I have to do is think I'm rich and speak it into existence, and it'll happen?!* Not exactly, but rather, this book laid out the steps required to turn your hopes and dreams into reality. Learning this simple yet powerful concept was the first of many to come.

For example, there was a time that I was constantly worried about money. I would focus on times when I felt the universe had taken money away from me. I had been putting out a negative vibration of loss and regret regarding money. I had a victim mindset. I wasn't being present. Instead of being grateful for the income I had, I wanted more but wasn't working harder to obtain it. I was resistant to the advice of family and friends who were trying to encourage me. it wasn't until I read a book on the ego, that I was able to gain an objective view of myself and receive the constructive criticism of others. No one can get through to you until YOU get through to you. Reading provided me with the inspiration to do this. So start reading! Even for just 10 minutes a day. You can even open up multiple books throughout the week, rather than reading one book from start to finish. This is something I do after I feel bored with a book I'm reading or it's getting redundant. I change it up by going to a different book, getting inspired, and eventually going back to that original book.

35

Here are some of my favorite personal development books:

- "The 5 Second Rule" by Mel Robins
- "The Alchemist" by Paulo Coelho
- "The Power of Now" by Eckhart Tolle
- "Your Erroneous Zones" by Wayne W. Dyer
- "The 7 Habits of Highly Effective People" by Stephen R. Covey
- "The Millionaire Mindset" by T. Harv Eker

Whatever piece of inspirational literature that you choose, you are not required to read it start to finish. I give you permission to read a few pages of a different book each morning. The point is to start your day with a little nugget of wisdom that you can carry with you throughout the day.

LIMB #3

MEDITATE

Meditating has been the most impactful part of my journey. Like I stated in the prologue, it takes time to experience the full benefits. If you're new to meditation, and you find it difficult to be still - you're not alone! We are human, and our minds have so much chatter. But when we allow space for our mind to observe our thoughts, you will be setting the stage for unlimited self-growth. Meditation begins as something you do alone, away from distractions. But as you learn in the eighth limb, meditation is the most powerful tool we have as we go about our day. The goal is to be in a state of constant meditation.

The point of meditation is to quiet the mind so that you can tune in to your true self that knows who you are and where you want to become. So how do you meditate? At first, the key to meditation is to focus on the breath. As cliché as that sounds, it's the best way to allow your mind to quiet. It's very therapeutic to pay attention to the breath, anyways. The entire time - make it the soundtrack of your meditation. If you don't live in a place where you can comfortably meditate outside, to hear the sounds of nature, then you may lightly play a soothing playlist of 432hz or music with no words. It will help the mind relax and raise positive vibrations. 432hz is the "frequency of the universe," which is instantly healing.

Meditation has been practiced for thousands of years, offering numerous benefits for mental and physical health. Regular meditation can significantly reduce stress levels, enhance emotional well-being, and improve overall quality of life. A study published in JAMA Internal Medicine found that mindfulness meditation programs can help reduce psychological stress, including anxiety and depression, in diverse adult clinical populations.

Beyond mental health, meditation positively impacts physical health. Research indicates that meditation can lower blood pressure, improve heart rate variability, and enhance immune function. A meta-analysis in the Journal of the American Heart Association concluded that meditation may be considered as an adjunctive therapy for cardiovascular risk reduction. Incorporating meditation into daily routines can lead to lasting improvements in well-being. Even short, consistent meditation sessions have been shown to yield significant benefits. As more individuals adopt this practice, the collective impact on public health could be substantial, underscoring the importance of meditation in modern life.

When I'm inside my home meditating, I personally put on a chakra cleansing playlist that I found on YouTube, that I later on found on Spotify. Each track in the playlist ignites and stimulates each individual chakra. I always start with the Root - and then move up the body from there. I believe it's very important to focus on opening up the chakras and tuning into the body to ensure you don't have any blockages. For many months, I was frustrated with how I was feeling and wasn't eating very well due to stress, and as soon as I sat down and meditated on the chakras (for an entire hour), I instantly was gifted with no more emotional eating. Something I had struggled with for years.

It was so relieving. I had just learned that night of focusing on them that I had blockages. My root and sacral chakras were so out of alignment. They were unbalanced because I wasn't taking the time to sit still. I was in a place where I was traveling a lot and allowing bad energy to touch me. As soon as I opened up these two chakras, I promised myself that I'd be low-key and focus on my own energy. This lasted five months. I'm forever grateful for this period of time to cleanse my energy.

Moral of the story - you may not know that you have some trauma in your energy locks. This is the major reason why so many people struggle with anxiety and depression. Meditating deeply allows the mind to reflect on what's truly going on. These are things that you can't figure out most of the time on your own.

Each morning, meditate for at least 10 minutes. Make it your goal to keep sitting until your eyes are glossy when you open your eyes. This takes me anywhere between 20-35 minutes. The longest I've sat down to meditate was an hour and a half, and this was the most enlightening experience I've had (it was during my 200 hour yoga teacher training). Each week, up your time by 5 minutes until you reach 45 minutes. If you feel called to go beyond that, more power to you! On the days you don't have the time to do so—at least get in 10 minutes. This strengthens your mind and carries off into your body and overall aura.

LIMB #4

GRATITUDE JOURNAL

"Gratitude is the healthiest of all human emotions. The more you express gratitude for what you have, the more likely you will have even more to express gratitude for." —Zig Ziglar

I can't remember the first day I started writing and speaking what I'm grateful for; all I know is that was the KEY to all my blessings. Writing down what you're grateful for is literally telling the universe you're ready for more. It's showing you deserve all that is given to you. The ones who aren't thankful and act ungrateful are never going to be as successful as those who are thankful.

Incorporating daily gratitude practices, such as maintaining a gratitude journal, can significantly enhance mental and physical well-being. Research indicates that individuals who regularly express gratitude experience improved mood, better sleep, and stronger relationships. For instance, a study by Emmons and McCullough found that participants who kept weekly gratitude journals reported fewer physical symptoms, felt better about their lives, and were more optimistic about the upcoming week than those who recorded hassles or neutral life events.

Real-life examples further illustrate the benefits of gratitude journaling. Oprah Winfrey, a prominent advocate of gratitude journals, has shared that this practice has been instrumental in maintaining her focus on life's positives, even during challenging times. She notes that consistently writing down things she is grateful for has helped her dramatically shift her perspective and appreciate the present moment. She wakes up and writes in her journal 3 things she's grateful for every morning and 3 things at night before she goes to bed. Before I even knew this, I had already been doing it, which was great confirmation that I was on the right path. My dream is to help myself and others to reach their full potential. Gratitude is a critical element of this process.

Moreover, gratitude journaling can foster resilience. By regularly acknowledging positive aspects of life, individuals may develop a more optimistic outlook, enabling them to cope more effectively with adversity. This practice encourages a focus on positive experiences and emotions, which can counterbalance negative thoughts and stressors; which we all can get caught up on at times of our lives. When thing after thing afters, it's almost like a wake up call to stay resilient through it all. Once you overcome the obstacles, you'll find presents for you at the end of the tunnel.

Be sure to be as specific as you can on what you're grateful for. Write down exactly who and what it is that lights you up so much each day. Write about everything that made you smile that day. Write as many small wins as you can. Close your eyes and re-visualize what it is that you're grateful for. This will help manifest more of these things into your life.

The attitude of gratitude will then become a habit - and you'll constantly stop and think to yourself how grateful you are. It's almost overwhelming sometimes, but always such a breath of fresh air. I feel like it's almost easy to forget how grateful we are if we don't make it a habit to think about it and express it. That's when memories fade away quicker because we didn't properly sit and just thank God for the moment.

When I first started practicing this, I wouldn't shut up about how grateful I was. I was a sunshine-loving, rainbow-shooting-out-of-my-ass 19-year-old with happy tears rolling down my face. It was nothing short of extra. I sometimes felt like I was 'too much' and held back my feelings on happiness to make sure I wasn't too much for anybody. I finally stopped caring, just about five years ago. Do not have shame for having gratitude all the time. Do not hold back overwhelming happiness. Let it shine when you have those moments, and choose to surround yourself with other like-minded people who are also a joy to be around. In summary, daily gratitude practices, particularly through journaling, offer a simple yet powerful tool for enhancing overall well-being, and will carry into your life beyond your imagination.

LIMB #5

SPEAK WORDS OF AFFIRMATIONS/MANTRAS

A few examples of affirmations are:

- I AM strong.
- I AM good enough.
- I AM beautiful inside and out.
- I AM perfect just the way I am.
- I AM love and light.
- I AM successful.
- I AM worthy of all my desires.
- I AM abundant.
- I AM thriving.
- I AM grateful.
- I AM worth loving.

A few examples of mantras are:

- Life is working in my favor.
- Good opportunities flow effortlessly to me.
- My aura is beautiful.
- I shine like a diamond.
- People are drawn to my energy.
- No person, place, or thing has any power over me unless I

give it.
- No one is me, and that is my greatest superpower.
- I am free to express my emotions.
- My smile lights up the room.
- I love every part of my body.
- I trust the universe to bring me my highest good.

Affirmations/mantras are positive statements that individuals repeat to themselves, aiming to challenge and overcome self-sabotaging and negative thoughts. This practice fosters a positive self-image and encourages a proactive mindset. Affirmations can activate the brain's reward centers, promoting positive changes in behavior and negative thought patterns into good ones. It's really so cool to think how simple this practice is, to speak kind things out loud, and write them down, to have long-lasting effects on the mind. However, being human often prevents us from seeing how easy something is when we get stuck in negative thought patterns. This is why I urge you to implement this practice into your daily morning routine. It will stop you in your tracks before you even get started. For those of you who struggle with this, you know what I mean.

The benefits of daily affirmations extend beyond mental health. They can improve problem-solving abilities under stress and enhance academic performance. A study published in PLoS ONE found that self-affirmation improved problem-solving performance in chronically stressed individuals, bringing their performance up to the level of those with low stress. This suggests that affirmations can serve as a buffer against the negative effects of stress, enabling individuals to perform at their best even under pressure.

To maximize the effectiveness of affirmations, it's essential to practice them consistently and with intention. Crafting affirmations that are personal, positive, and present-tense can make them more impactful. For example, statements like "I am confident and capable" or "I embrace challenges as opportunities for growth" can reinforce a positive self-concept. Over time, these affirmations can reshape thought patterns, leading to lasting improvements in self-esteem and resilience.

A mantra is a statement that is true or may not be true yet—but you keep speaking it until you believe it with all that you have until it comes true. This statement can be something like *I am a bestselling author*, or *my success is inevitable* (these are a couple of mine I have been speaking into existence!). Your daily words of affirmation and mantra practice can be anything that will remind you of how you want to be. Mantras are powerful, and the more you write and speak them, the more you will notice them to become true. Sometimes you need to "fake it until you make it." Be bold and ambitious. Craft mantras that direct you toward your highest goals. Make a vision board and print the mantras to attach to the board where you see them daily. Sometimes the fear of success is just as impairing as the fear of failure. Don't let this fear stop you.

Think of things that you really want but you may not think you deserve. Speak them. Speak with confidence and with conviction, and write these things down as another entry in your Magic Morning journal. I would like to challenge you to speak these mantras daily for a month and see how next month goes. I guarantee that you'll have spoken at least one of these things into existence. This will empower you by showing how in control you are of your destiny. The world does not shape you; you shape the world. Other people will see these things, as well. This isn't a fake theory. It has actually been scientifically proven. Sigmund Freud, psychologist and influential thinker of the early twentieth century, demonstrated that self-affirming statements truly change what you believe. He elaborated on the theory that the mind is a complex energy-system. As a result, how you walk into a room will change. You will stand taller, be more 'put together,' and begin to have the most powerful feeling of self-love. This will ultimately manifest your dreams into reality by becoming the person you're meant to be for that specific dream or goal.

Once you get the hang of this exercise, you'll be speaking anything and everything into existence. It's just a matter of having conviction in whatever you're speaking. This is also true in the reverse! You can speak negativity into existence! Saying you're not good enough or thinking someone else doesn't like you, etc..will increase the likelihood of this becoming a reality.

Positive thoughts = positive life. Negative thoughts = negative life.

LIMB #6

VISUALIZATION

Hello to your new best friend: Visualization! This concept is actually pretty new to me in the last few years, but it's what truly pieced it all together for me. Whenever I'm nervous about a certain meeting or event, I meditate, visualizing how I want things to go. Always focus on what you want; never focus on what you don't want. Visualization of the positive outcome forces your mind to push away the possible adverse outcomes.

Visualization is a powerful technique that involves creating vivid mental images of desired outcomes, serving as a corner-stone of the Law of Attraction. This practice is based on the premise that focusing on positive images and emotions can attract corresponding real-life experiences. Research supports the efficacy of visualization in goal attainment. For instance, a study published in the Journal of Consulting Psychology found that participants who engaged in mental imagery of their goals were more likely to achieve them compared to those who did not utilize such techniques.

The Law of Attraction says that like attracts like, suggesting that positive or negative thoughts bring about corresponding experiences. While empirical evidence on the Law of Attraction is limited, the concept aligns with psychological principles such as the self-fulfilling prophecy, where an individual's expectations influence their behavior, leading to the anticipated outcome. A review in the Journal of Personality and Social Psychology highlights how positive expectations can enhance performance and well-being.

Incorporating visualization into daily routines can enhance motivation and focus. Techniques such as creating vision boards or engaging in guided imagery can help individuals clarify their goals and maintain a positive mindset. As I already noted, creating a vision board to display somewhere in your home, that reminds you of your dreams, desires, and mantras, will help you exponentially in your growth. By consistently visualizing desired outcomes, individuals may increase their likelihood of success, as the practice reinforces commitment and aligns subconscious behaviors with conscious objectives.

Before writing the first edition of this book (that was about 1/4 of the length, only sold to my followers 5 years ago), I took the time to visualize my dream life, such as my future husband, my dream house, and where I wanted to be in 5 years. Well, here I am, LIVING MY MANIFESTATIONS! I have my dream house, my dream partner, one beautiful daughter and one growing in my belly, with financial freedom—just as I visualized five years ago. I am a living testament to this theory.

For me, this is a very powerful exercise, and sometimes brings me to tears of joy because of how clearly I can see what I want to come true. It's so amazing. Stop where you are and try this visualization exercise:

Begin by coming to your breath, in a comfortable seated position or laying down, and close your eyes...

Start imagining yourself walking through whatever it is you want to live closest to (i.e. the beach, a jungle, an open field). Imagine yourself walking along through the path and pay attention to if it's sunny, or if there are animals around, or sweet-smelling flowers. Allow yourself to be grateful for those things in your vision. Now keep walking until you come close to your dream house. Stop and take a moment to appreciate the hard work you've put in to own this home. Now start to imagine what it looks like, what car might be parked in the driveway, what pets (if any) are present, and even friends/clients/family that are there.

The first time I did this, I spent a good 30-40 minutes living my dream life in my mind. It was so clear. I teared up the whole time. I encourage you to spend this much time doing this at least once a month when it comes to the future. For all the other days of visualizing, I urge you to think about whatever tasks you need to get done, and having positive, happy days. Also, when it comes to feeling your best in your skin...visualize where you want to be and where you are in the current moment and just smile at all the parts of you that you love. We all have flaws, but our flaws are what make us beautiful...believe it or not. So appreciate them as much as you appreciate the good things about you.

LIMB #7

MOVE YOUR BODY

This was the first thing I was able to make a daily habit. It changed my life into an endorphin-loving, positive fairy land! Exercising and yoga brought me in tune with my body more than anything else. At first, I didn't enjoy the exercise, but I did enjoy how I felt afterwards. But as I continued moving my body, I started to enjoy the exercise itself. My body started to crave it! The endorphins that exercise gives you is the feeling of euphoria. This feeling is sometimes called the 'runner's high' if you're a runner. You also get this feeling with other forms of movement, though. I never understood it until I felt it.

Incorporating daily exercise into one's routine, even in brief sessions, offers substantial health benefits. Engaging in physical activity for as little as five minutes can positively impact cardiovascular health. A study published in Circulation found that replacing five minutes of sedentary behavior with vigorous activities, such as running or stair climbing, resulted in clinically significant reductions in both systolic and diastolic blood pressure.

Beyond cardiovascular improvements, regular exercise enhances mental well-being. Physical activity stimulates the production of endorphins, leading to improved mood and reduced symptoms of anxiety and depression. Additionally, exercise promotes better sleep quality, which is essential for overall health. Consistent physical activity is crucial for those aiming to lose or maintain a healthy weight. Even if you eat well, our bodies truly need movement. Regular exercise helps control weight by utilizing calories that would otherwise be stored as fat. Moderate-intensity activities, such as walking, can also contribute to weight management, so it doesn't have to be a high intensity workout to reap the benefits. Plus, this means you can eat more of the foods your body loves and craves. Exercise means your metabolism works quicker, allowing you to take in more calories to repair your muscles. The food will be used as energy for your next movement session, rather than stored as fat.

For me, the best time to work out is in the morning. It's a way to jump start all the energy for the rest of the day after breathing and speaking your intentions. Choose 4-5 days per week to engage in your favorite form of exercise. If you workout at night, or have a schedule that fits a different time slot for exercise, that's fine, too. When you don't exercise, dedicate this time to a restorative type of movement, such as stretching, massage, or mild yoga.

I suggest that you have a variety of go-to exercises to change it up every week. This will ensure your body doesn't get too used to a certain form of movement, plateauing your growth. Personally, I love at-home workouts. I'll queue up a workout video on YouTube and follow along. Sometimes, I find it more enjoyable to workout with friends. The motivation from someone else does so much on days when you might not be feeling your best. The point is that making exercise a part of your daily routine will increase your confidence and drive to SLAY THE DAY and all of your goals.

Shaping my body has given me full control over how I feel when I look at myself. We all have control! It's just about putting time away every day to work on it. After whatever form of movement you choose to do, the best part of it all is rewarding yourself with a well-deserved shower! I imagine all of the old parts of me being rinsed away by the water. It's so soothing to me. I encourage you to close your eyes and imagine your fears doubts being rinsed down the drain.

Your doubts, negativity, old habits… let them be rinsed away with this shower. It's a beautiful way to stop and actually FEEL the water hitting your skin and appreciate the sensation instead of taking it for granted. Same thing goes for when you wash your hair and body. Wash it with love. Take your time and really put love into whatever you're washing. It's that extra compassion towards yourself that makes the biggest difference. This is making time to love yourself more. In summary, dedicating time each day to physical activity, whether a few minutes or a full hour, can lead to significant improvements in both physical and mental health. Establishing a daily exercise routine is a proactive step toward a healthier and more fulfilling life.

* * *

Now you see, with the countless number of scientific references I mentioned, alongside personal experiences—Incorporating a morning routine that includes gratitude journaling, affirmations, visualization, movement, and reading is more than just a practice—it's a transformative experience. These habits work together to set a positive tone for your day, grounding you in gratitude and purpose while energizing your mind and body. By beginning each morning with intentionality, you cultivate a mindset of abundance and resilience that carries you through challenges and opportunities alike. Affirmations remind you of your worth, mantras allow you to become who you want to be, visualization clarifies your goals, movement awakens your energy, and reading expands your knowledge and perspective. This combination empowers you to show up as your best self every day, reinforcing the belief that small, consistent steps can create powerful, lasting change in your life. The morning is your foundation—build it strong, and the rest of your life will follow suit.

5

Live your Purpose

Is your current job something you're not passionate about? Does it take you a lot of effort to get ready to go to work? If you don't love what you do every day, it's going to be difficult live an authentic life. If you don't like your work, then you're most likely working and socializing with people that you don't have much in common with other than the fact they're also working for a paycheck.

A sense of purpose provides direction and meaning. We feel more fulfilled and motivated when we align our actions with our values and passions. Purpose doesn't have to be grand or life-changing; it can be found in small acts, like helping others, learning something new, or working toward a personal goal. Practice: Reflect on your values and goals. Consider what activities make you feel alive and fulfilled. Set an intention to incorporate these into your life, and take small, consistent steps toward them.

Living with purpose involves aligning daily actions with one's core values and long-term goals, leading to a more fulfilling and meaningful life. Research indicates that individuals with a strong sense of purpose experience numerous benefits, including improved mental health, increased longevity, and enhanced well-being. For instance, a study published in *Psychology Today* found that having a purpose in life is associated with better physical health, mental health, and happiness.

Self-reflection is essential for discovering and living one's purpose. Engaging in activities that resonate with personal passions and strengths can provide insight into what brings joy and satisfaction. Additionally, setting meaningful goals and pursuing them with intention can foster a sense of purpose. As noted in *Greater Good Magazine*, cultivating positive emotions like gratitude and awe can help individuals focus on how they can contribute to the world, thereby finding purpose.

Moreover, living with purpose often involves contributing to causes greater than oneself. Volunteering, mentoring, or engaging in community service can provide a sense of belonging and fulfillment. According to Harvard Health Publishing, having a sense of purpose is linked to a lower risk of death from various causes, especially cardiovascular disease and blood conditions.

Everyone—including you—can find work that they're passionate about. So many people get caught up in the comfort and security of a steady paycheck, yet they lose sight of their passion and purpose. Many of us don't even know what our passion is due to social pressures, like being a successful doctor or lawyer. You may have spent most of your adult life in university just to graduate and have a degree in something you hate doing or that takes up most of your free time. You may have never sat down to think about what you'd actually like to spend your life doing if it weren't for your programming on money.

Finding what excites you most is a process. It's a journey on which we embark on this beautiful quest to personal development. It's all about following your intuition. If you get the feeling that there must be more, that's the universe giving you the sign you need to leave what you're doing and continue the search.

Stay open and available to the opportunities that are presented to you, especially if they are out of your comfort zone. Entering situations that make us uncomfortable or afraid is the only way to grow. I promise that most of your fears are just in your mind. When you take a leap-of-faith, you will find that you can handle much more than you think you can. Things that you were once afraid of will turn into things that excite and challenge you. This is my main advice to you: Say YES to the opportunities that scare you!

For example, before becoming a yoga teacher, I worked for four years as a hairdresser in a salon. I enjoyed this work, but I kept getting the feeling that there was something more for me. I kept thinking that I could do something more challenging and required my true, authentic self. Sure, I was good at doing hair, but my skills and passions weren't fitted to be spent in the beauty industry for the rest of my life. Salons were pretty toxic, in my experience, and it brought me down. It can be a superficial environment. I wanted to travel and be my own boss. This wouldn't be possible if I remained an employee of a salon.

One day, the urge to travel and seek adventure grew so strong that I booked a 6-week European trip, 6 months in advance! This both excited and terrified me. But it forced me to find a way to get that time off and to save up the money required to embark on this journey. I often find that if I put myself in a situation where I MUST work hard and plan to succeed, I always rise to the challenge. This strategy might work for you, as well.

After five months of hard work, I had saved up enough money for the adventure. But I had to quit my job in order to get the time off that I needed. This was terrifying! But I had committed myself financially to the decision to travel. This was the motivation I needed to stay the course and follow through with my decision. What steps can you take to commit yourself to an adventure that scares and excites you?

Always work your hardest and have a good attitude, even if you don't love what you're doing. Sometimes, HOW you do something is just as—if not more—important than WHAT you do. Even though I didn't love my job at the hair salon, I did try my hardest every day. I always did the best job I could and had the best attitude I could muster. As a result, I had formed good relationships with all of the clients I had at the salon. When I returned from traveling, I had no money and no job. I knew I didn't want to go back to the salon. I knew I had the discipline to motivate myself to work hard and make my own work schedule. I was proactive, contacted all of my previous clients, and offered to charge them the same amount as they had paid at the salon, but I would drive to them! Since I had worked so hard with such a good attitude at the salon, nearly all of the clients agreed to this arrangement. Soon, I had my own little hair clientele. This allowed me to make a more flexible work schedule for myself, which then allowed me to travel on the weekends, spend more time with friends and family, and to engage in activities that interested me.

One day, I tried a yoga class, and then another, and then another. Before I knew it, I was hooked, and I started looking into how I could practice yoga for a living while still being my own boss. Like most people my age, I was active on Instagram. I would post photos of the progress I was making in my practice, which was received positively, and I began gaining a following. A little light bulb turned on in my head. I started following fellow yogis on Instagram who inspired me and had a large social media following. Many were traveling to beautiful places while getting paid to tag their favorite companies in their posts. This was my dream job! "But how can I make this dream a reality?" I asked myself. In order to make this dream a reality, I knew I needed to pay attention to other successful influencers in my niche and follow what has worked for them.

As the saying goes, "A journey of a thousand miles begins with a single step." So, I finally listened to my intuition. One day, at the end of a yoga class, I found myself crying tears of joy because I knew that I had found my passion. I wanted to dedicate my life to learning and sharing the practice of yoga. That very day I signed up for yoga teacher training.

When you are pursuing your passion, the Universe will often send you messages of confirmation, letting you know that you're on the right path. The very same week that I signed up for Y.T.T., the most unbelievable thing happened: An NFL athlete on the Detroit Lions messaged me, asking if I could be his private yoga instructor. He asked me this purely based on what he saw and read on my Instagram feed. Ironically, I was still in a place of self-doubt. Whenever I'd put up a new post, part of me felt I wasn't good enough: my body wasn't perfect, and my poses weren't advanced enough. I was still in a chapter of my journey where I'd compare myself to other yogis.

Imagine if I had listened to that voice, that inner critic that is always feeding you negative thoughts about yourself and the world? If I had followed my inner critic instead of my intuition, the excellent opportunity to become a professional athlete's yoga coach to many more to come would have never happened! So follow your intuition and your positive inner voice, and ignore the inner critic who is always trying to keep you from growing.

Soon after I began teaching this pro athlete, I was referred to several others. The Universe sent me lots of positive feedback, and things were moving fast. Not even one month later, I was offered a paid trip to California to shoot several full-length yoga classes for several days. This opportunity paid for my yoga teacher training, plus extra to go to my savings. All this happened during my yoga teacher training, something I had signed up for impulsively after that overwhelming sign from God.

These kinds of opportunities weren't normal, and I knew that. I knew that God or the universe was sending me abundance for making the right decisions by following my intuition. Everything I was hoping for was coming to fruition. I know this is a pretty crazy story, but it happened. And it can happen to you, too. But you must listen to your intuition, visualize what you want to manifest, and then GO FOR IT!

Whatever it is that you've always wanted, take some time now to sit with your dreams and VISUALIZE them coming to life. Make this today's meditation.

6

Brand Yourself

E mbarking on a self-love journey is integral to personal development and plays a pivotal role in effective personal branding. Understanding and valuing oneself lays the foundation for authentic self-presentation, which is essential in building a personal brand that resonates with others. Personal branding is about knowing and valuing yourself, and then broadcasting that to the world. This process involves recognizing one's unique strengths, values, and passions, and aligning them with one's higher purpose.

Choosing a path that aligns with your higher purpose requires introspection and a clear understanding of your core values and long-term goals. The Harvard Business School Online emphasizes that personal branding is the intentional, strategic practice of defining and expressing your value. By aligning your personal brand with your higher purpose, you create a cohesive narrative that not only defines who you are but also guides your decisions and actions toward meaningful outcomes.

Incorporating self-love into your personal branding strategy enhances authenticity and fosters trust with your audience.

When you genuinely appreciate and express your true self, it attracts opportunities and relationships that are in harmony with your higher purpose. *Brandingmag* notes that personal brand narratives involve self-assessment and strategic content creation, which are essential in building a brand that reflects your true self. This alignment not only contributes to personal fulfillment but also establishes a strong, authentic presence in your professional and personal life.

In this day and age, if you want to be your own boss, then chances are you need to brand yourself. Your brand can be made from anything you enjoy doing and whatever you're good at. This doesn't mean you have to be an entrepreneur if you don't want to. You can still brand yourself and call in opportunities if you work a regular job. This also has to do with your beliefs and morals. In the world of social media, branding yourself is the most important thing you can do if you want to be offered opportunities based on the content of your posts. I have been posting about my journey to self-love for the past 10+ years. This is why I've decided to write a book about self-love and personal development, to ultimately match me with other people wanting to find the same things in life. Although I post about many different topics, from yoga to travel to motherhood and beyond, the common thread that runs through them all is the philosophy of self-love. I live and breathe it, because it makes life so much more beautiful.

You can only love yourself if you are being your authentic self. And your authentic self is your brand! Sit down and really think about what you believe in. Ask yourself:

64

1. What is most important to me?
2. What message do I most want to share with people?
3. What cause, or causes, do I feel most called to fight for?
4. If you didn't care what your friends and family thought, what would you stand for?

Let go of fear. Envision your happiest self and start living your true brand. This might make you choose more things and people that align with your lifestyle. This might make you quit your job and move across the country! Whatever you feel called to do will probably scare you at first. It's time to start being honest with yourself about WHO you are and WHAT you want. Not about what the people you surround yourself like and want in life. This happens a lot if you stay friends with people you grew up with just for the fact that you've known each other for a long time. Or you spend a lot of time with family who may have certain views on things that you've just tagged along with. You want to reflect about the things you truly believe in, and don't change your views on it just because everyone around you thinks differently. An example of this is U.S. politics today. I won't go into that, but most people just choose who they vote for depending on who their peers are voting for.

In summary, branding yourself is very important, both professionally and in your personal life, to align yourself with the right people and opportunities. You can take this advice to live your dream life of becoming your own boss, or simply use it to pave your own path in life.

7

Manifestation

Although I've talked about it a lot already, I can't stress enough about the power of manifestation. Whatever you focus on the most is what comes into being. If you focus on achieving success, then you will find success. If you focus on *avoiding* failure... you may not fail, but you won't find success! If you are determined to achieve success, then failure will actually be a good thing! We can only learn through failure. We can only discover what will work after discovering what doesn't. If you are not determined to achieve success, then you will give up as soon as you fail. Manifesting the life you want requires commitment and hard work.

Manifestation, the practice of bringing one's desires into reality through focused thought and intention, has garnered significant attention for its potential to influence personal outcomes. Rooted in the Law of Attraction, it reveals that positive or negative thoughts can attract corresponding experiences into one's life. While some view manifestation as a metaphysical concept, emerging scientific research offers insights into its psychological underpinnings.

Neuroscientific studies suggest that visualization and positive affirmations can activate brain regions associated with motivation and goal-directed behavior. For instance, a study published in Social Cognitive and Affective Neuroscience found that self-affirmation activates the brain's reward centers, enhancing an individual's ability to adapt to challenging situations. This indicates that regularly focusing on positive outcomes can prime the brain to recognize and seize opportunities aligned with one's goals.

Moreover, psychological research supports the efficacy of manifestation techniques. A study in the Journal of Personality and Social Psychology demonstrated that individuals who engaged in mental simulations of successful outcomes were more likely to achieve their goals compared to those who did not. This suggests that deliberate focus on desired results can enhance motivation and performance, thereby increasing the likelihood of success.

Incorporating manifestation practices into daily routines, such as visualization exercises and positive affirmations, can foster a proactive mindset. By consistently aligning thoughts and emotions with desired outcomes, individuals may not only enhance their psychological resilience but also create a conducive environment for personal and professional growth.

During your Magical Mornings, visualize your path to success. Visualize what failures may occur and then visualize *how you react* to these failures. Visualize yourself getting up, dusting yourself off, and continuing forward with the valuable lessons you learned from the failures. Let go of doubt and fear. Fear will cause you to view failure as something fatal to your success. When, in fact, it is quite the opposite: failure is *required* to achieve success. You will never find a successful person who hasn't experienced multiple failures. Manifestation is real, but it requires a tolerance to failure. You can only manifest the life that you have committed yourself to achieving.

Live as if you already have what you want. Every time I want something, I imagine myself already having it and act as if I already have it. I believe that I deserve it. Then, more times than not, within weeks, I'll be in a position to acquire what I wanted. We're made of energy. Energy attracts like energy. It's really that simple. Manifestation is about embodying and emitting the energy that you want to receive. Writing in your journal daily will help you manifest your desired dreams. The more often you envision it coming into reality, the more likely it will.

8

Trust in the Universe

You must know that everything you're doing is going to pay off. Sometimes it may seem like it's not going to, especially when things aren't going exactly as planned. A lot of times, Source will give you some bumps on the road right before magic happens. This is to test you. You must not lose faith. Have patience and remain optimistic, rain or shine.

For example, I started thinking about writing this book about 8 months before I actually started writing it. I was super excited, visualizing how my brand was going to take off once I started producing written material. But so many obstacles kept coming up that drained me of my motivation. Then, I started worrying and overthinking every aspect of the writing process. I had no idea how to put together something like this because I had never done it before.

Then came the distractions: relationships and work that pulled me in different directions. It took me a good 6 months to finally sit at my computer and start. I found that I didn't have the patience required to learn all the technical aspects of producing a book. Finally I just opened up my Notes app and started writing! I wrote and wrote and wrote until I had all of my table of contents written out, my preface, and the first two chapters. JUST LIKE THAT!

I knew that this was the project I wanted to dedicate my time to, and I told God that 8 months prior. I was being tested by all the distractions that had been sent my way. I dedicated my time to this project. So, whenever something came up each week, I prioritized my time much better. I learned that whenever I get overwhelmed by a project, I just need to start! Once you start something, the universe begins to support you.

There's always something to do and somewhere to be with family and friends, but sometimes you just need to focus on *your* goals and put in the work. This is when trusting in the universe comes in handy: When you don't know if all your hard work is going to pay off, trust that IT WILL! This is when you must have faith. As part of your Magical Morning Meditation, ask God for peace, patience, and discipline as you pursue your dreams. Trust that all that you want is going to come in time.

9

Flow State & Going with the Flow

T he more in harmony you are with the flow of your own existence, the more magical life becomes. - Oprah Winfrey

Going with the flow invites us to embrace as it unfolds, without rigidly clinging to expectations or attempting to control every outcome. This mindset allows you to respond to challenges and opportunities more easily, fostering a sense of harmony in your daily life. This was huge for me as a control freak. Psychologists suggest that people who adopt a "flow mindset" often experience reduced stress levels, as they're able to adapt to shifting circumstances rather than resisting change. In fact, research in Frontiers in Psychology shows that going with the flow promotes psychological flexibility, which is linked to higher resilience and emotional well-being.

This approach is especially valuable in today's fast-paced, unpredictable world, where unexpected changes can easily disrupt plans. When you practice "going with the flow," you become more comfortable with uncertainty, allowing you to enjoy life's spontaneity rather than feeling overwhelmed by it. Practicing gratitude for life's small surprises and approaching each situation with an open mind can help nurture this mindset. Adopting a "flow" approach doesn't mean passivity; instead, it's about actively engaging with life as it unfolds, creating a more peaceful, adaptable, and even magical experience.

Achieving a state of flow, often described as being "in the zone," involves complete immersion in an activity, leading to heightened focus and enjoyment. Psychologist Mihály Csíkszentmihályi, who introduced the concept, noted that flow occurs when one's skills are well-matched to the challenges faced, resulting in a harmonious experience. This alignment not only enhances performance but also contributes to a more fulfilling and "magical" life, as individuals find deeper satisfaction in their pursuits. Doing things you love helps you get into this flow! For me, it's easy to get into flow state while I write, produce content for my YouTube channel demonstrating yoga, showing my travels... However, in the modern world, where most people work at a job with a boss who may not treat them very well, it can be harder to get into this flow state. It's not impossible, but just harder. Mentioning branding yourself earlier was to bring attention to possibly open the idea to expand your life a bit by calling in more opportunities to achieve success in a niche you actually enjoy, for more inner peace and happiness.

The "going with the flow" philosophy complements the flow state by encouraging adaptability and openness to experiences. By relinquishing excessive control and allowing life to unfold naturally, you can reduce stress and cultivate a sense of peace.

This approach aligns with all the mindfulness practices I've shared thus far, emphasizing present-moment awareness and acceptance. Numerous studies, as referenced, indicate that such practices can improve mental health and overall happiness.

Integrating both the flow state and the principle of going with the flow into daily life can lead to transformative experiences. Engaging fully in activities that align with personal passions while remaining open to life's unpredictability fosters resilience and joy. This balance allows individuals to navigate challenges gracefully, enhancing the richness and "magic" of their life journey.

As soon as I began believing that everything would work out for me, I decided to "go with the flow." I trusted that everything that happened, good or bad, was supposed to happen. I trusted that it was all leading me in the right direction. It made me accept everything for what it was, rather than being upset for something I had no control over.

I used to be in funks that lasted weeks on end, where I was stuck on something that happened to me. That was my problem... nothing happened *to* me. They were out of my control and not aimed at me. That internal switch changed everything for me. This switch ended my downward spirals of negative emotions. I am human, though, so negative emotions will still come. The difference now is that I keep track of my cycles and I go with the flow of the emotions. I don't fight them, but instead I take them in stride and process them each day with reflection. I ask myself, "Why did that person trigger me?" or "I'm just in my feelings, I'm probably overreacting." I can then walk out into the world with the same amount of confidence and resilience that I have on my best days. I don't try to fight what life throws at me. Whether the universe presents me with negative or positive emotions, failure or success, I go with the flow.

One of my favorite books, 'Yes Man' by Danny Wallace, taught me the importance of saying YES. The book is about a man who decided to say "yes" to every opportunity that was handed to him for an entire year. So many wonderful adventures came as a result. Although I haven't take it as far as he did in the book, I still say yes to so many more things than I used to. Before, I'd say no for the silly reason of not feeling pretty that day or because I didn't feel like being social. Now, I usually say yes to work and social opportunities, *especially* if I'm not feeling my best. No matter how I feel, the energy I have and the worthiness that I offer are far greater than my appearance or emotional state. Afterwards, I'm always glad that I said yes. When we go with the flow of "yes" rather than the "flow of no," we can interrupt our negative thought cycles.

YOU HAVE SO MUCH TO OFFER. And there are so many amazing opportunities out there if you just live with confidence, even if you have to "fake it 'til you make it." This is exactly what I did, and as a result I have found myself flowing into the best situations. They call it living in a 'flow state' for a reason!

10

Positive Body Talk

lright, enough talk about the universe and waking up early. Let's get into another essential aspect of self-love: BODY TALK. So many people, women *and* men, go through life hating their physical bodies. As I stated before, thinking negatively towards ANYTHING causes you to send a negative frequency towards that thing.

A scientific experiment was conducted that illustrates this principle. Masaru Emoto, a Japanese researcher, conducted experiments to explore the power of thought and intention on water. Emoto's research involved exposing water to various thoughts, words, and music and then freezing it to observe the crystal formations. He claimed that positive words and intentions resulted in beautiful, symmetrical crystals, while negative words led to disordered, asymmetrical crystals.

He also performed the experiment on rice. The goal was to show what effects emotions had on a sprouting grain of rice. He put rice into three different air-tight jars and labeled one of them 'LOVE,' the second one 'HATE,' and the third one 'IGNORED.' To the jar labeled 'love' he spoke words of love. To the jar labeled "hate," he spoke hateful words. And the third jar he ignored. After three weeks of this, the jars of rice were compared. The rice in the jar that was spoken to with love became pink and had a sweet aroma. The rice in the jar spoken to with hate became dark and foul-smelling. The rice in the jar that was ignored remained white but smelled bad. This study has been tested hundreds of times, and every time, it's the same end result. How does that make you feel?! How do you talk to your body? Read that again.

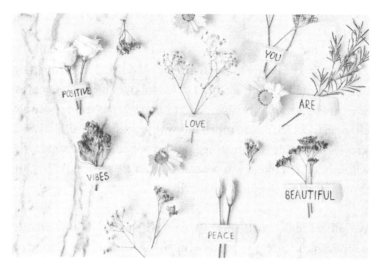

This study made me come to tears, thinking back to all the times I had thoughts of hatred toward my body. Could you think of the damage it was doing? Positive words of affirmation towards your body are a MUST. If you want to flourish and glow from the inside out, you must speak kindly to your body. No hatred, no ignoring, only positivity.

This changed my body so much. I started telling my body how much I love it. I would record videos of myself (and still do) of me looking at myself in the mirror, smiling, and saying to my body, "I love you. You're beautiful. Thank you for taking care of me." I would do this every time I needed to be cheered up. Our body is the vessel that holds our soul. The fact that you are alive is a miracle. Billions of cells, biological processes, and neuronal connections must be working together in beautiful harmony in order for you to stay alive. Think about that when you think of your body. And speak to it only words of love and gratitude.

This is how I broke free from the negative self-talk regarding my body. I turned something that I obsessed over in a negative way and turned it into a positive. As a result, I started seeing positive changes: exercise was more enjoyable and more effective, I saw less bloating after eating, and I stopped binge eating. My whole body felt like it was working better because it WAS! Our thoughts affect the physical world.

We all struggle with this. It can be hard to admit what's happening inside our heads. But that's one of the reasons I wrote this book. I'm here to help you get whatever you may not love about yourself off your chest, write it down in your journal, and turn it into something beautiful. Don't wish death upon yourself like in the rice experiment. Make it your goal not to live a life of self-hate and regret. Instead, focus on how you will live a life in which you love your body. And be grateful for the miracle that it is.

I want you to write a journal entry right now, and label it, 'Day 1 of Loving every inch of my body.' I want you to write down every feature you love about yourself and then look in the mirror or even try recording yourself as you look at every feature that you *think* is imperfect. Then, say nice things about these features. Whatever it is, be super specific and smile really big when you look at yourself. Say you're sorry for all the times you harmed it with negative thoughts.

As silly as this may seem, make it a habit and soon you'll feel happiness when you look in the mirror. You will begin to manifest the body you want, and you will start to fall in love with every feature. You are one of a kind. You have no flaws! You may look different than other people, but that's because we're all unique: everyone looks different! "Flawless" runway models and gorgeous actors constantly admit that they don't like their bodies. They're just like you! So start loving your body and everything that make it unique!

11

Let Go of Doubts

D oubt. You know, that little voice in your head that shows up every time you're making a decision? The one that you usually listen to and then regret it later? This is part of being a human. Doubt pops up most prominently whenever you're making a decision that scares you. It often comes about because, deep down, you don't believe that you deserve it. Like applying for a certain position at your dream job. Or actively promoting your business to people you meet. But you can learn to ignore this voice. It helps to write down what you wanted in the moment right after a decision was presented to you. What was your instant gut reaction?

I want you to write down some doubts you've had recently or in the past that prevented you from going for something you wanted. Then, write down what decision you would have made if you knew you wouldn't have failed. In the future, that is the decision you should always make, and you should remember this as a reminder to stop listening to the negative thought processes that you revert to.

Self-doubt is a pervasive feeling that can significantly impact one's mental health and overall well-being. When individuals consistently question their abilities and worth, it can lead to increased anxiety, depression, and a diminished quality of life. Research indicates that low self-esteem is closely linked to mental health issues; for instance, a study found that individuals with low self-esteem are more susceptible to depression and anxiety disorders. The effects of self-doubt extend beyond mental health, influencing various aspects of daily life.

Persistent self-doubt can hinder personal and professional growth, as individuals may avoid pursuing opportunities due to fear of failure or inadequacy. This avoidance can result in missed chances for advancement and fulfillment. Moreover, self-doubt can strain relationships, as individuals may struggle with trust and communication, further isolating

83

themselves and exacerbating feelings of loneliness. Addressing self-doubt is crucial for fostering a healthier mindset and improving one's quality of life. Engaging in positive self-talk and affirmations can help reframe negative thought patterns. For example, practicing affirmations like "I am capable and deserving of success," as you should have already practiced in the chapters before this, can bolster self-esteem and counteract self-doubt. Additionally, seeking support from mental health professionals or support groups can provide valuable strategies and perspectives to overcome self-doubt if you can't seem to shake it yourself.

For example, whenever I am invited to a party or event, I get super excited about it and tell myself, "Okay Mel, you're going to have so much fun at this event!" but then hours go by. The clock is ticking to get ready, and my limiting beliefs come creeping in: "I don't look good today," "I don't have anything to wear," "I have no one to go with," etc. Does this sound familiar? Whether you're an extrovert or an introvert, you'll feel energized after attending the event. However, the doubts will cause a lot of you to stay home half the time. The fact is, we're all human. We will never feel "perfect." But if you ignore the doubts and go with that first choice that you made, it will strengthen your intuition.

Conversely, if you make the choice that your doubt favors, you'll miss out on the blessings that the universe is trying to send you, like meeting someone who could benefit your business or meeting and connecting with a group of like-minded people. I'm constantly contending with doubt. It's hard work. But with the help of the journaling and meditation practices that I've talked about, I'm gaining power over them daily. Doubts will always be there, but as you practice switching your mind to benefit your best self, they will become easier and easier to ignore.

In summary, while self-doubt is a common experience, its impact on mental health and daily life is profound. You can cultivate a more confident and fulfilling life by recognizing and actively addressing self-doubt through positive affirmations, choosing your initial thoughts, or seeking extra support.

12

Let Go of Expectations

One of the surest ways to sabotage your journey to self-love is to have expectations. One of my favorite sayings is, "Happiness equals reality minus expectations." In other words, don't have expectations that are too grand; otherwise, you won't be happy because your hopes are never matching reality! Everything will feel like a hopeless fight—and it will be!

Letting go of expectations is crucial to enhancing mental well-being and fostering healthier relationships. Rigid expectations can lead to feelings of disappointment, frustration, and resentment when outcomes do not align with preconceived notions. A study published in the Journal of Personality and Social Psychology found that individuals with high expectations often experience greater dissatisfaction due to unmet anticipations, which can negatively impact their overall happiness and life satisfaction.

Moreover, holding onto unrealistic expectations can strain

interpersonal relationships. Expecting others to behave in specific ways or fulfill certain roles can lead to conflicts and misunderstandings. Research indicates that couples who maintain flexible expectations and adapt to changing circumstances report higher levels of relationship satisfaction. A study in the Journal of Marriage and Family found that adaptability in expectations contributes to more harmonious and enduring partnerships.

Practicing mindfulness and acceptance can aid in releasing rigid expectations. Mindfulness encourages individuals to focus on the present moment without judgment, reducing the tendency to cling to specific outcomes. Acceptance involves embracing situations as they are, rather than how one thinks they should be. Implementing these practices can lead to reduced stress and increased emotional resilience. A study published in Behaviour Research and Therapy demonstrated that mindfulness-based interventions significantly decrease anxiety and depressive symptoms by promoting acceptance and reducing attachment to expectations.

If you have expectations about how your life should go, how others should behave, etc. then you're living with a sense of entitlement. Entitlement is the arrogance to believe that you deserve everything you want and that you know it's going to come to you. The Universe hates entitlement and loves those who are humble, hardworking, and who go with the flow. If you have expectations, then you are not going with the flow because you think you know what is best for you, and you're just waiting for your version or reality to come true. We do not know exactly what we need. The Universe does. You must surrender to a power that is greater than yourself.

Shoot for the moon, land among the stars

So, how can you have dreams but not have expectations? It may seem impossible. But it's not. Here's how: First, aim at a goal your intuition says is right for you, but don't aim at a realistic goal in your mind. Our minds sometimes hold us back from what's possible because there are an exponential amount of possibilities in life. Just like my favorite saying goes: "Shoot for the moon. Even if you miss, you'll land among the stars." At their root, your dreams should be the desire to allow Source to lead you to your passions and purposes; on the moon or the stars. The point is that the higher you set your goals, the more room you have to be much more wildly successful than you already are. Don't expect to reach the exact goal you set. You will get somewhere close to that, or sometimes even get more than you ask for. The point is to lose the expectations, but don't stop dreaming big even if you don't get exactly what you ask for.

Meditate on this. Look at your hopes, dreams and goals and allow yourself to let go of any expectations that they will come to pass. Come to this present moment and allow yourself to feel gratitude and happiness for what is. Envision yourself remaining present throughout your journey to self-love and open to what the universe is telling you along the way.

You must also release expectations that you have of friends, parents, siblings, lovers, etc. Life is complicated and unpredictable. Accept this. People will let you down, and lovers and friends will be lost. If your peace of mind depends on an outside relationship, it's only a matter of time before your world comes crashing down. The only relationships that you have control over are the relationship that you have with yourself and the relationship that you have with Source. If you love yourself, and trust in the higher energy guiding you on your journey, then you will always have peace of mind. No one can give you anything you can't give yourself. Re-read that line again! The moment you let go of expectations is the moment you'll be set free.

13

Living with Childlike Joy

Honoring my Dad's spirit to teach you all how to live a little more adventurously and choose to focus on the positives in life

My dad's laughter and silliness could fill a room, and his energy was as vibrant as it was contagious. He had this incredible ability to make happiness his only mission, living each day with childlike wonder and boundless excitement. He didn't just want to live; he wanted to experience life to the fullest, doing the things that kept him feeling young, alive, and in love with every moment. Growing up with that kind of energy was like having a front-row seat to the art of living joyfully. Carrying on his legacy is one of my greatest purposes. I strive to bring that same spark, that same zest for life, into my own experiences and to pass it along to my children. To embrace life's wonder and chase new adventures with an open heart—these aren't just memories of my dad; they're lessons he gifted me, and they guide me every day. This chapter is dedicated to finding that childlike happiness within ourselves, honoring the child we once were, and keeping that innocence and excitement alive.

Remembering the Joyful Child Inside You

As adults, we often lose touch with the carefree, joyful parts of ourselves—the parts that once lived in awe of the world around us. My dad taught me that we never really lose our child selves; they're always within us, waiting to be remembered. Think back to who you were as a kid. What made you laugh? What made you feel fearless, curious, and alive? Reconnecting with those memories reminds us of the pure, unfiltered happiness we all once had.

Take a moment to close your eyes and picture yourself as a child. What were you excited about? What were the dreams you held close? Let that young version of yourself serve as a reminder of your capacity for happiness.

Nurturing Your Inner Child

My dad's happiness wasn't just about doing fun things (which he was really good at!); it was also about loving and caring for himself with kindness and compassion. He honored his inner child by giving himself permission to play, laugh, and be curious. We can do the same by treating our inner child as we would any child—with patience, acceptance, and encouragement. Speak to yourself as you would a young child. Offer yourself words of kindness, especially during difficult times. Take care of the "baby version" of you who deserves love and nurturing. Imagine you're holding that younger self close, reassuring them that they're worthy of joy and happiness. If you're a parent, you intuitively treat your children with overabundant amounts of nurturing and love. Treat yourself the same way!

Embracing Childlike Happiness

Happiness can feel elusive in adulthood, but sometimes it's as simple as embracing the little things that make us feel young. My dad chased adrenaline and excitement, whether it was through sports, adventures, or spontaneous trips. It kept him vibrant and full of life, and it's a spirit I want to carry with me always. Finding childlike happiness is about letting ourselves enjoy the world around us without overthinking it. Getting outdoors as much as possible, or going to hangout with your friends without making excuses.

Practice: Make time for activities that spark your curiosity and excitement. Try something new, engage in a playful activity, or revisit something you loved as a child. Give yourself permission to be joyful without worrying about "acting your age." This is always more fun with people, so try new classes or go to that thing a friend or family member has mentioned they enjoy doing. It puts us out of our comfort zones and you might find a new hobby or new group of friends in the process!

Ask yourself: "What would make my child self happy?" One of the best ways to find fulfillment is by asking ourselves what our younger selves would want. As kids, we had dreams and desires that were unburdened by the stresses and limitations of adulthood. Embracing that childlike perspective helps us reconnect with what truly makes us happy. Think back to your childhood dreams. What did you want to do, to be, or to experience? Incorporate those desires into your life now, honoring your child self and keeping their dreams alive. My dad always told me I could do anything I wanted in life, and to choose things that make me happy. Hearing that at a young age really stuck with me, I truly listened to him. He was my hero.

Chasing Adventure and Adrenaline

My dad's passion for life was fueled by adventure and a love for adrenaline. Whether it was snowboarding, wakeboarding, karate, snowmobiling, random trips with his friends, or simply laughing until he was out of breath, he understood that life was meant to be felt deeply. One memory that I saw him do countless times, was him sitting on a lawn chair looking out at the lake I grew up on, with a cup of coffee or a beer, saying, "Life is good!" He loved music and drumming with his fingers and making other people smile. That is a quality of someone who has self-love which pours into everyone else.

He showed me that true happiness comes when we're willing to take chances and seek out experiences that make us feel alive. He'd always rush me out of the house to go do something fun. Or wake me up early to hit the lake before anyone else was out there. There was no waves and we loved going really fast. It made me feel so alive and I know him seeing me happy made him feel more alive as well. Living with this sense of adventure allows me to honor his legacy and embrace life with the same fearlessness he embodied.

Practice to not shy away from experiences that challenge you or bring out your adventurous side. Try something that pushes you beyond your comfort zone, and see how it reignites that spark within. You're never too old to feel the thrill of something new.

Teaching These Concepts to the Next Generation

As I carry my dad's legacy within me, it's important to pass these values along to my children. I want them to know that happiness is more than a fleeting emotion; it's a way of living. By embracing their own curiosity, joy, and adventure, they can lead lives that are rich and fulfilling. Showing them how to live in wonder, how to nurture their inner child, and how to chase after the things they love is one of my greatest responsibilities as a parent.

Practice with Kids: Encourage your children to express themselves freely, to ask questions, and to explore the world with curiosity. Take time to laugh with them, play with them, and show them the beauty of living fully.

Living His Legacy

Living with joy, adventure, and curiosity isn't just about honoring my dad; it's about carrying the happiness he infused into life. As his daughter, I know that the best way I can live his legacy is by keeping that spark alive in myself and sharing it with others. I already am a lot like him, which I'm so grateful for. My soon-to-be husband always tells me he loved my dad so much because he sees me in him. I want my children— and everyone who crosses my path—to feel the energy he left behind. To live each day with a heart wide open, to let laughter be their guide, and to find happiness in the simple, beautiful things in life. In the end, true happiness is about living in a way that honors the child within us, the child we were, and the joy we can still create. We all deserve to live with that sense of wonder, to let our spirits stay young, and to make each day a little brighter. My dad showed me that, and now it's my purpose to pass it on.

Rest in heavenly peace, angel

14

Conclusion

I n the journey of self-love and happiness, we've explored practices, mindsets, and insights that create a foundation for a more purposeful, peaceful, and fulfilled life. Each chapter in this book represents a layer of that foundation— a stepping stone toward understanding and embracing your worth, living authentically, and cultivating a life that aligns with your highest self. Self-love is not a single act; it's a commitment, a daily choice, and a journey of unfolding—and happiness is a choice we can all make each day.

Beginning with affirmations and positive self-talk, we saw how words can shape our reality. "I am" statements anchor us to the truth of our inner strength and potential, reminding us that we have the power to redefine ourselves from within. Practicing gratitude and documenting our blessings brought us closer to appreciating the present, allowing us to move through life with more joy and resilience. These simple habits accumulate into lasting change, grounding us in positivity and abundance.

We also explored the importance of going with the flow, learning to let go of rigid expectations and surrendering to the present moment. This adaptability is liberating, allowing us to experience life with less frustration and greater appreciation. Living in alignment with our purpose, visualizing our goals, and embracing the power of manifestation reinforced our journey by focusing our energy on creating a life that feels both intentional and magical.

We remembered what it felt like to be a child with more playfulness, excitement, and adventure. It isn't about having a perfect life; it's about choosing to see the beauty in the imperfections, embracing the adventure in the unknown, and keeping a sense of wonder alive no matter your age. Living with childlike joy means giving yourself permission to play, dream, and laugh—reminding yourself that life is meant to be experienced, not just endured. By focusing on the positives, we shift our energy toward what truly matters: connection, love, and the moments that take our breath away. When we live more adventurously, with curiosity and excitement, we honor not only the child within us but also the legacy of those who taught us how to embrace life fully.

Alongside these mental shifts, we integrated the benefits of daily exercise, mindfulness, and early rising to anchor these practices into our daily routine. These habits remind us that self-love is also a physical practice, one that respects our body and our time. By embracing our mornings and making space for movement and reflection, we pave the way for a day infused with clarity and strength.

This book encourages you not only to embrace these practices but to remember that self-love is a path to self-discovery. It's about recognizing your worth, celebrating your uniqueness, and living each day as an opportunity to become more authentically you. In moments of doubt, remember the tools you've gathered here—the affirmations, visualizations, moments of gratitude, and mindful practices. They are here for you, guiding you back to your center and encouraging you to live a life led by love.

As you go forward, may you hold space for the journey of self-love and happiness with compassion and patience. You are worthy of the love you give yourself, and as you continue to nurture that love, you'll find it spilling into every corner of your life. Remember that self-love is a practice, one that you can return to over and over again, each time discovering new depths and insights.

On the next page, there is a sample of the Magical Morning worksheet that brings the eight limbs of self-love together in the form of an interactive meditation. I hope that you find it useful and that you'll use it every morning. If you haven't already, I encourage you to buy a journal that is aesthetically pleasing to you. One that excites you to see, hold and write in.

I am grateful for each and every one of you who purchased this book. I hope that it's a door that introduces you world of self-love. If no one has told you yet today, you are worthy and loved!

* * *

THE MAGIC MORNING

I AM:
  MY WHY:
  What I read today:
  What came up during my meditation:
  What am I grateful for today?
  My affirmations/mantras:
  What mantras did I speak today?
  How did my body feel during my workout/recovery session?

* * *

MY MAGIC MORNING:

As an example, I have provided one of my Magic Morning journal entries below.

I am a powerful manifestor . I have created such a blessed life for myself. I am resilient and strong; yet beautiful and soft at the same time. I am independent and choose my reality every single day. I am free.

I'm here to inspire and teach others how to live out of love. I help people find self-love by first loving myself. I want to live a life full of experiences without guilt. I am here for a reason.

I read 'The 7 Habits of Highly Effective People' this morning and gained insight on the power of discipline. I'm constantly reminded that my choices around my magic morning are working for the best and because of this, I will always be successful.

I am at awe of tears that rolled down as I meditated. I am one with the universe, as the universe is inside of me. Constantly being held. I am on my path. I am peace. I am love. I am light.

I am grateful that I have a voice in a world full of billions of people. I am grateful for my body and all that it can do. I am grateful for my friends and family, who always check in with me.

I am love. I am light.

* * *

Afterword

Reviews are gold, just as feedback is a gift! If you've enjoyed this book, would you consider rating it and reviewing it on Amazon? Originally written 5 years ago, but finally formatted and extended for Amazon—thank you to all the supporters for the long wait. This book is 3x as long, and I had to honor my dad's life since he's why I am back on my path to publishing and living my purpose. RIP to the best dad a girl could ever ask for. I'm grateful you're guiding me to the things I forgot I loved.

FEEDBACK IS A GIFT

My goal is to positively impact as many people as I can. Your feedback will help me, help more people. As I stated earlier, We can only love others as much as we love ourselves. I hope that this book will help you to love yourself and find greater joy and purpose in life. If it does, pay it forward and share this guide with your friends, family, and anyone you feel it could benefit.

Also, feel free to practice your Magic Mornings with your friends. Do the exercises separately, then come together and discuss what you learned and experienced. Cultivating self-love is one of the most important things you can do for yourself, and helping others along their self-love journey is one of the most important things you can do for them. Two heads are better than one. And the best way to learn something is to teach it. I'm forever thankful for my friends, because we uplift each other and help keep each other accountable for personal growth.

Best of luck! Xoxo

Resources

Ardelles. (2024, November 5). The power of words: How language shapes our reality. Retrieved from https://ardelles.com/the-power-of-words-how-language-shapes-our-reality/

Brandingmag. (2023). Personal brand narratives: From self-assessment to strategic content. Retrieved from https://www.brandingmag.com/gidyon-thompson/personal-brand-narratives-from-self-assessment-to-strategic-content/

Brown, B. (2010). The gifts of imperfection. Hazelden Publishing.

Byrne, R. (2006). The secret. Atria Books.

Carver, C. S., & Scheier, M. F. (1990). Origins and functions of positive and negative affect: A control-process view. Journal of Personality and Social Psychology, 58(4), 665–676. https://doi.org/10.1037/0022-3514.58.4.665

Cascio, C. N., O'Donnell, M. B., Tinney, F. J., Lieberman, M. D., Taylor, S. E., Strecher, V. J., & Falk, E. B. (2016). Self-affirmation activates brain systems associated with self-related processing and reward and is reinforced by future orientation. Social Cognitive and Affective Neuroscience, 11(4), 621–629.

https://doi.org/10.1093/scan/nsv136

Centers for Disease Control and Prevention. (2022). Benefits of physical activity. Retrieved from https://www.cdc.gov/phy sicalactivity/basics/pa-health/index.htm

Creswell, J. D., Dutcher, J. M., Klein, W. M., Harris, P. R., & Levine, J. M. (2013). Self-affirmation improves problem-solving under stress. PLoS ONE, 8(5), e62593. https://doi.org/ 10.1371/journal.pone.0062593

Crisis Text Line. (2024). 100 positive affirmations for better self-care. Retrieved from https://www.crisistextline.org/blo g/2024/01/08/100-positive-affirmations-for-better-self-car e/

Csíkszentmihályi, M. (1990). Flow: The psychology of optimal experience. Harper & Row.

Davidson, R. J., Kabat-Zinn, J., Schumacher, J., Rosenkranz, M., Muller, D., Santorelli, S. F., … & Sheridan, J. F. (2003). Alterations in brain and immune function produced by mindfulness meditation. Psychosomatic Medicine, 65(4), 564–570.

EatingWell. (2024). Got 5 minutes? Do this exercise to help lower blood pressure, new study says. Retrieved from https://w ww.eatingwell.com/5-minutes-exercise-blood-pressure-stud y-8742275

Elrod, H. (2012). The miracle morning: The not-so-obvious secret guaranteed to transform your life (before 8AM). Hal

111

Elrod.

Emmons, R. A., & McCullough, M. E. (2003). Counting blessings versus burdens: An experimental investigation of gratitude and subjective well-being in daily life. Journal of Personality and Social Psychology, 84(2), 377–389. https://doi. org/10.1037/0022-3514.84.2.377

Emoto, M. (2004). The hidden messages in water. Atria Books.

Goyal, M., Singh, S., Sibinga, E. M., Gould, N. F., Rowland-Seymour, A., Sharma, R., & Haythornthwaite, J. A. (2014). Meditation programs for psychological stress and well-being: A systematic review and meta-analysis. JAMA Internal Medicine, 174(3), 357-368. https://doi.org/10.1001/jamainternmed.201 3.13018

Harvard Business School Online. (2023). Personal branding: What it is and why it matters. Retrieved from https://online.h bs.edu/blog/post/personal-branding-at-work

Harvard Health Publishing. (2019, November 28). Will a purpose-driven life help you live longer? Retrieved from https://www.health.harvard.edu/blog/will-a-purpose-drive n-life-help-you-live-longer-2019112818378

James, A. (1903). As a man thinketh. Collins.

Kabat-Zinn, J. (2003). Mindfulness-based interventions in context: Past, present, and future. Clinical Psychology: Science and Practice, 10(2), 144–156. https://doi.org/10.1093/clipsy.

bpg016

Levine, G. N., Lange, R. A., Bairey-Merz, C. N., Davidson, R. J., Jamerson, K., Mehta, P. K., & Smith, S. C. (2017). Meditation and cardiovascular risk reduction: A scientific statement from the American Heart Association. Journal of the American Heart Association, 6(10), e002218. https://doi.org/10.1161/JAHA.1 17.002218

Maslow's Theory of Human Behavior: A comprehensive exploration of needs and motivation. (2024, September 22). NeuroLaunch. Retrieved from https://neurolaunch.com/masl ows-theory-of-human-behavior/

Mattingly, S. M., Martinez, G., Young, J., Cain, M. K., & Striegel, A. (2022). Snoozing: An examination of a common method of waking. Sleep, 45(10). https://doi.org/10.1093/sleep/zsac184

Mayo Clinic. (2022). Exercise: 7 benefits of regular physical activity. Retrieved from https://www.mayoclinic.org/healthy-lifestyle/fitness/in-depth/exercise/art-20048389

Neff, L. A., & Karney, B. R. (2004). How does context affect intimate relationships? Linking external stress and cognitive processes within marriage. Journal of Marriage and Family, 66(2), 348–362. https://doi.org/10.1111/j.1741-3737.2004.0 0025.x

Personal Branding Blog. (2023). Know your worth: Empower-ment through personal branding. Retrieved from https://ww w.success.com/know-your-worth-why-building-a-personal-

113

brand-is-an-act-of-self-empowerment/

Psych Central. (2022). How to go with the flow in life: 12 tips. Retrieved from https://psychcentral.com/health/ways-to-go-with-the-flow-and-stay-in-the-moment

Psych Central. (2022). The relationship between low self-esteem and depression. Retrieved from https://psychcentral.com/depression/is-low-self-esteem-making-you-vulnerable-to-depression

Rogers, C. (1959). A theory of therapy, personality, and interpersonal relationships as developed in the client-centered framework. Psychology: A Study of a Science, 3, 184–256.

Science of People. (2024). Gratitude journal: 35 prompts, templates, and ideas to start. Retrieved from https://www.scienceofpeople.com/gratitude-journal/

Selig, M. (2021, August 23). 10 powerful benefits of living with purpose. Psychology Today. Retrieved from https://www.psychologytoday.com/us/blog/changepower/202108/10-powerful-benefits-living-purpose

Self-determination theory. (2024, October). Wikipedia. Retrieved from https://en.wikipedia.org/wiki/Self-determination_theory

Seppala, E. (2018, May 17). Seven ways to find your purpose in life. Greater Good Magazine. Retrieved from https://greatergood.berkeley.edu/article/item/seven_ways_to_find_your_

purpose_in_life

Sleep Foundation. (2022). Benefits of waking up early. Retrieved from https://www.sleepfoundation.org/sleep-hyg iene/benefits-of-waking-up-early

Surmount Global. (2023, March 15). The transformative power of "I AM" statements: Shaping your reality with positive affirmations. Retrieved from https://www.surmountglobal.o rg/post/the-transformative-power-of-i-am-statements-shap ing-your-reality-with-positive-affirmations

Taylor, S. E., Pham, L. B., Rivkin, I. D., & Armor, D. A. (1998). Harnessing the imagination: Mental simulation, self-regulation, and coping. American Psychologist, 53(4), 429–439. https://doi.org/10.1037/0003-066X.53.4.429

Vetter, C., & Daghlas, I. (2021). Association of sleep timing with risk of major depressive disorder. JAMA Psychiatry, 78(7), 731–739. https://doi.org/10.1001/jamapsychiatry.2021.0959

About the Author

With over a decade of experience in yoga and holistic wellness, Melinda has touched the lives of thousands through her classes, online content, and personal coaching. She combines her extensive knowledge of yoga, somatic therapy, and mindfulness practices to empower her audience to lead healthier, more fulfilling lives. As a devoted mother and entrepreneur, Melinda understands the challenges of balancing a busy lifestyle with personal well-being and is committed to guiding others on their journey to self-discovery and inner peace. Join her newsletter for book updates, classes, free offerings, and inspiring words.

You can connect with me on:

- ⊕ https://www.melspirations.com
- ⓕ https://www.facebook.com/melspirations
- ⌐ https://www.instagram.com/melspirations

Subscribe to my newsletter:

✉ https://subscribepage.io/melspirations

Made in the USA
Coppell, TX
29 November 2024

41277798R00075